I0605373

AMERICA'S ETHNIC DIVERSITY

BLACK AMERICANS

by Emma Kaiser

BrightPoint Press

San Diego, CA

© 2026 BrightPoint Press
an imprint of ReferencePoint Press, Inc.
Printed in the United States

For more information, contact:
BrightPoint Press
PO Box 27779
San Diego, CA 92198
www.BrightPointPress.com

ALL RIGHTS RESERVED.
No part of this work covered by the copyright hereon may be reproduced or used in any form or by any means—graphic, electronic, or mechanical, including photocopying, recording, taping, web distribution, or information storage retrieval systems—without the written permission of the publisher.

LIBRARY OF CONGRESS CATALOGING-IN-PUBLICATION DATA

Name: Kaiser, Emma, author.
Title: Black Americans / by Emma Kaiser.
Description: San Diego, CA: ReferencePoint Press, 2026 | Series: America's Ethnic Diversity | Audience: Grade 7 to 9 | Includes bibliographical references and index.
Identifiers: ISBN: 9781678210984 (hardcover) | ISBN: 9781678210991 (eBook)
The complete Library of Congress record is available at www.loc.gov.

CONTENTS

AT A GLANCE

- Black Americans make up about 14 percent of the US population.
- Many Black Americans are descendants of Africans who were forcibly brought to America through the slave trade.
- Slavery officially ended in the United States in 1865. But Jim Crow laws continued to deny Black Americans the same rights as white Americans.
- The Civil Rights Movement worked to gain equal rights for Black Americans. Some leaders of the Civil Rights Movement included Martin Luther King Jr. and Malcolm X.
- Black Americans have contributed to every area of American culture, from language and art to fashion and style trends.

- The Harlem Renaissance (1918–1937) was a time of great artistic output from the Black community. During this time, literature, music, and dance from Black artists became recognized around the world.

- Disparities still exist between Black and white Americans across nearly every area of society. These disparities exist in wealth, health, education, and more.

- Protests against racial injustice and inequality were sparked after George Floyd's murder in 2020. These protests have helped bring new attention to the ways racism still exists.

CELEBRATING BLACK HERITAGE

Ada and her family walked onto the National Mall in Washington, DC. It was packed with people. The White House was hosting a concert. Famous soul singer Gladys Knight sang for the crowd. Patti LaBelle and others performed, too. They were all celebrating Juneteenth.

Juneteenth is short for "June 19th." President Abraham Lincoln signed the Emancipation Proclamation on

On June 10, 2024, the White House hosted a concert to celebrate Juneteenth.

January 1, 1863. This marked the end of slavery being legal. But the news did not reach all enslaved people right away. The Union army arrived in Galveston Bay, Texas, on June 19, 1865. The army announced the end of slavery. More than 250,000 enslaved people lived in Texas. They gathered to

President Joe Biden made Juneteenth a national holiday on June 17, 2021. Juneteenth is also known as Emancipation Day or Freedom Day.

celebrate their freedom. Celebrations continued on that day throughout the years. The holiday became known as Juneteenth.

Juneteenth had become a federal holiday in 2021. Now the White House was hosting a celebration. Ada saw America's first Black, female vice president give a speech. Kamala Harris said, "As we celebrate Juneteenth, together we are reminded of the promise of America. A promise of freedom, liberty, and opportunity, not for some but for all."[1]

DIVERSITY IN AMERICA

Juneteenth is important to Black American culture. Ada and her family are Black Americans. About 14 percent of Americans identify as Black. The United

WHERE BLACK AMERICANS LIVE

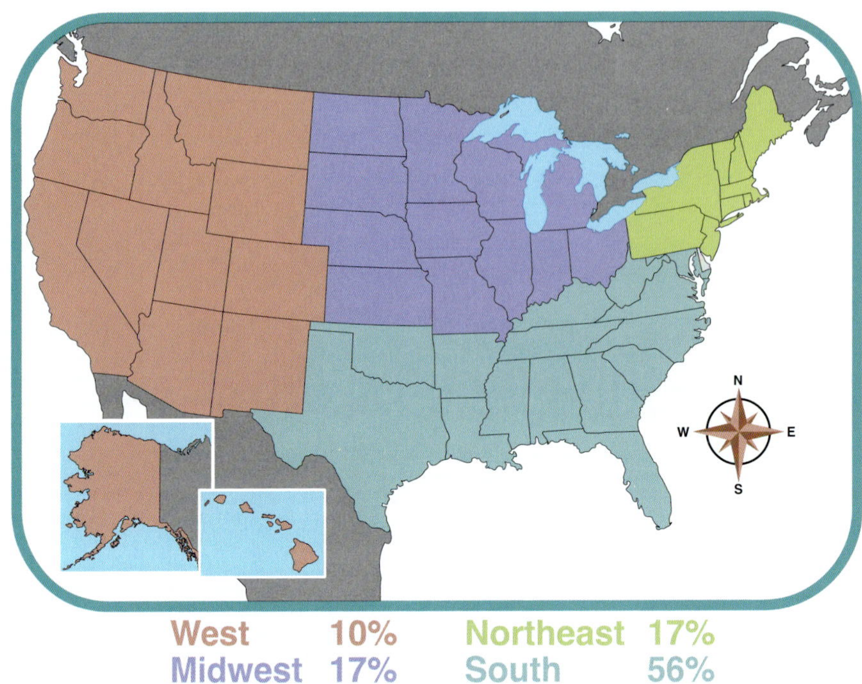

Source: Mohamad Moslimani et al., "Facts About the US Black Population," Pew Research Center, *January 18, 2024. www.pewresearch.org.*

The Pew Research Center used 2022 census data to determine what percentage of Black Americans lived in different regions. The data includes Black, multiracial Black, and Black Hispanic people.

States is home to people of many different races, ethnicities, and cultures. *Race* describes people who share physical traits, such as skin color. *Ethnicity* describes people who have a shared cultural identity.

Black Americans are part of the United States' ethnic diversity.

Black Americans may be born in America. They may also be **immigrants** from other countries. Many Black Americans have African heritage or are descendants of enslaved Africans. But not all Black Americans share this history. Much of Black Americans' history includes hardship, oppression, and injustice. But it's also a story of resilience, achievement, and celebration.

CHAPTER ONE

HISTORY OF BLACK AMERICANS

The first known Black person in the modern-day United States was Juan Garrido. In 1513, he joined Spanish explorer Juan Ponce de León. They went on an expedition to Florida. Garrido was a free man. Spanish settlers founded Saint Augustine, Florida. It was North America's first permanent European settlement. Freed and enslaved Africans worked in the settlement.

Saint Augustine, Florida, was home to the first Black Americans.

DRIVE
RESERVED
FOR

A sign at Fort Monroe National Monument in Hampton, Virginia, marks the 1619 arrival of the first Africans to English North America.

In 1619, a group of twenty to thirty enslaved Africans landed in Virginia. This was an English colony. Some enslavers treated their slaves like indentured servants. Indentured servants worked for a certain number of years. When their time was up, they were freed. Some European settlers came as indentured servants. English and Spanish settlers also enslaved

Native Americans. However, settlers began to treat African people differently. Employers refused to release Black workers from servitude. They came up with false reasons why Black people were inferior. They used these excuses to keep Black people enslaved. By 1750, slavery was legal in all English colonies.

Landowners needed workers for their land. The demand for enslaved people grew. Europeans kidnapped Western Africans. They took them to North America. Slave traders held slaves in chains beneath the decks of slave ships. The conditions were brutally harsh. Millions died during the journey across the Atlantic Ocean. European and American ships brought approximately 12.5 million enslaved people to the Americas through the slave trade. Slave traders brought around 430,000 African people to the United States.

Enslaved people had no rights. They were treated like property. They were not allowed to learn to read or write.

SLAVERY IN THE UNITED STATES

Slave labor became the foundation for the new US **economy**. Most enslaved Africans and their descendants were forced to work on plantations in the South. These plantations grew crops such as tobacco, sugar, and cotton. Slavery was not common in the North. But the North still benefited from slave labor.

America gained independence from Great Britain after the

Enslavers often separated families by selling family members to other enslavers.

Revolutionary War (1775–1783). At that time, slavery became illegal in the northern states. But it remained legal in the South. The slave trade officially ended in 1808. But this did not end slavery. Plantation owners continued to buy and sell Black people who were already enslaved. Because new Africans were not being forced into slavery, enslavers forced slaves to have as many children as possible.

Thousands of enslaved people ran away to northern states. **Abolitionists** organized a network of routes and hiding places. This became known as the Underground Railroad. Some Black people found freedom in the North. But they still weren't treated equally. They didn't have the same rights as white citizens. Many were at risk of being kidnapped and sold back into slavery.

Tensions grew between the North and South. Much of the conflict revolved around whether slavery should continue. Abraham Lincoln was elected president in 1860. Lincoln did not want slavery to expand to new states or territories. The South feared Lincoln would give too much power to the North. In response, the South withdrew from the United States. This started the US Civil War (1861–1865).

Southern states created the Confederate States of America. The North became known as the Union. More than 186,000

Almost 200,000 Black soldiers served in the Union army and navy. At first, Black soldiers were paid less than white soldiers. In 1864, Congress passed a law granting equal pay, equipment, and supplies to Black soldiers.

ABRAHAM LINCOLN AND HIS

Emancipation Proclamation

Whereas On the Twenty-second day of September, in the year of our Lord one thousand eight hundred and sixty-two, a Proclamation was issued by the President of the United States, containing among other things the following, to-wit:

"That on the first day of January, in the year of our Lord one thousand eight hundred and sixty-three, all persons held as slaves within any State, or designated part of a State, the people whereof shall then be in rebellion against the United States, shall be then, thenceforward and forever free, and the executive government of the United States, including the military and naval authority thereof, will recognize and maintain the freedom of such persons, and will do no act or acts to repress such persons, or any of them, in any efforts they may make for their actual freedom.

"That the executive will, on the first day of January aforesaid, by proclamation, designate the States and parts of States, if any, in which the people thereof respectively shall then be in rebellion against the United States, and the fact that any State, or the people thereof, shall on that day be in good faith represented in the Congress of the United States by members chosen thereto at elections wherein a majority of the qualified voters of such State shall have participated, shall, in the absence of strong countervailing testimony, be deemed conclusive evidence that such State and the people thereof are not then in rebellion against the United States."

Now, therefore, I, ABRAHAM LINCOLN, President of the United States, by virtue of the power in me vested as Commander-in-Chief of the Army and Navy of the United States in time of actual armed rebellion against the authority and government of the United States, and as a fit and necessary war measure for suppressing said rebellion, do, on this first day of January, in the year of our Lord one thousand eight hundred and sixty-three, and in accordance with my purpose so to do, publicly proclaim for the full period of one hundred days from the day the first above mentioned order, and designate as the States and parts of States wherein the people thereof respectively are this day in rebellion against the United States, the following, to-wit:

ARKANSAS, TEXAS, LOUISIANA (except the parishes of St. Bernard, Plaquemines, Jefferson, St. John, St. Charles, St. James, Ascension, Assumption, Terre Bonne, Lafourche, St. Mary, St. Martin, and Orleans, including the city of New Orleans), MISSISSIPPI, ALABAMA, FLORIDA, GEORGIA, SOUTH CAROLINA, NORTH CAROLINA and VIRGINIA (except the forty-eight counties designated as West Virginia, and also the counties of Berkley, Accomac, Northampton, Elizabeth City, York, Princess Ann and Norfolk, including the cities of Norfolk and Portsmouth), and which excepted parts are, for the present, left precisely as if this Proclamation were not issued.

And by virtue of the power and for the purpose aforesaid, I do order and declare that all persons held as slaves within said designated States and parts of States are and henceforward shall be free; and that the executive government of the United States, including the military and naval authorities thereof, will recognize and maintain the freedom of said persons.

And I hereby enjoin upon the people so declared to be free, to abstain from all violence, unless in necessary self-defence, and I recommend to them that in all cases, when allowed, they labor faithfully for reasonable wages.

And I further declare and make known that such persons of suitable condition, will be received into the armed service of the United States to garrison forts, positions, stations and other places, and to man vessels of all sorts in said service.

And upon this act, sincerely believed to be an act of justice, warranted by the Constitution, upon military necessity, I invoke the considerate judgment of mankind, and the gracious favor of Almighty God.

In testimony whereof, I have hereunto set my name, and caused the seal of the United States to be affixed.

L.S. Done at the City of Washington, this first day of January, in the year of our Lord one thousand eight hundred and sixty-three, and of the Independence of the United States the eighty-Seventh.

By the President: ABRAHAM LINCOLN.

WILLIAM H. SEWARD, Secretary of State.

NOTE.---The rest of the slaves were afterwards freed by Legislation and Constitutional Amendments.

An artist's edition of the Emancipation Proclamation shows Abraham Lincoln with figures representing Justice and Liberty along with the Proclamation text.

Black soldiers fought for the Union Army. They did not receive equal pay. But they helped the Union win the war. Lincoln signed the Emancipation Proclamation in 1863. This document officially made slavery illegal. The war ended in 1865.

POSTWAR STRUGGLES

Nearly 4 million Black people were freed from slavery at the end of the war. The Thirteenth Amendment to the Constitution was added in 1865. This amendment states, "Neither slavery nor involuntary servitude, except as a punishment for crime [for which a person has been] convicted, shall exist within the United States."[2] The Fourteenth Amendment allowed citizenship for Black Americans. It was added in 1869. The Fifteenth Amendment was added in 1870. It gave Black men the right to vote. They could also run for office. Between 1869 and 1901, twenty Black citizens became US representatives and two became US senators.

However, many people refused to follow these new laws. Black people faced violence and **discrimination**. Southern states passed laws that outlawed interracial marriage. Jim Crow laws **segregated** all public places. This meant that Black people had separate schools, bathrooms, and more. White people also worked to keep Black Americans from voting. They intimidated those who tried to vote. They passed discriminatory laws to keep them from voting.

THE FIGHT FOR CIVIL RIGHTS

In 1954, the Supreme Court ruled that segregated schools were illegal. In 1957, Black students tried to attend previously segregated schools in Little Rock, Arkansas. But white mobs attacked the students. Local law enforcement blocked

Elizabeth Eckford (center) was one of nine students to desegregate Little Rock Central High School in 1957. These students became known as the Little Rock Nine.

the students from going to school. The US government sent federal troops to protect the students.

Black Americans fought against unfair laws. Civil rights leaders demanded new laws and protections. Black citizens organized **boycotts** and peaceful protests. But many protesters faced violence, arrests, and bombings.

The NAACP

NAACP stands for the National Association for the Advancement of Colored People. It was formed in 1909. The NAACP was led by Black leaders such as W.E.B. Du Bois and James Weldon Johnson. It brought attention to racial injustice. It fought for equal treatment in education, employment, housing, and more.

The March on Washington for Jobs and Freedom took place on August 28, 1963.

One of the most famous Civil Rights Movement leaders was Martin Luther King Jr. In 1963, King addressed a crowd of 250,000 people. They were gathered at the Lincoln Memorial in Washington, DC. This event became known as the March on Washington. It helped pass the Civil Rights Act of 1964. The act made racial discrimination illegal. Further protests and demonstrations led to the Voting Rights Act of 1965. This made it illegal to stop or discourage Black voters.

WORKING FOR EQUALITY

Black Americans experienced more legal protection. But they were still treated unequally. Leaders such as Malcolm X pushed for more Black teachers

Barack Obama served as US president from 2009 to 2017.

and improvements in Black education. Affirmative action programs helped Black students get admitted to higher education. Affirmative action also helped in job hiring. Black Americans could be fairly considered for jobs.

Despite centuries of adversity, Black Americans have contributed to US society in incredible ways. Black Americans built the foundation of the nation. They have fought in wars, worked for just laws, and served in the highest government positions. Barack Obama was the first Black president. He was elected in 2008. In his victory speech, he said, "Our union can be perfected. And what we have already achieved gives us hope for what we can and must achieve tomorrow."[3]

CHAPTER TWO

CULTURE AND TRADITIONS

Black culture is diverse. It's a blend of influences from many countries, ethnicities, languages, and traditions. Together these form a unique culture in the United States.

Many aspects of Black American culture have African roots. These are the languages, beliefs, and traditions that enslaved Africans brought with them. Some traditions survived. But enslavers worked

Black Americans come from a variety of backgrounds.

hard to erase this heritage. Descendants of enslaved Africans created their own culture. It was based on shared history and experiences.

Sometimes the terms *African American* and *Black* are used interchangeably. But they are not the same. Not all Black

Kwanzaa

Kwanzaa is a nonreligious holiday. It lasts for 7 days in December. An African studies professor named Maulana Karenga created it in 1966. The purpose of Kwanzaa is to celebrate Black Americans' history, values, community, and culture. It is mainly celebrated in the United States. Each day of Kwanzaa is celebrated by lighting a candle. The candles represent the seven principles of Kwanzaa. These include unity, purpose, and creativity.

Americans can trace their lineage back to Africa. Of those who can, many cannot trace to specific countries. Celeste Watkins-Hayes is an African American studies professor. "Part of what was stolen, when we think about slavery, . . . was that lineage," she says. "[People might say] 'I don't even feel comfortable claiming *African*, because I don't know the story of where my people have come from.'"[4]

Black Americans also include Black people who immigrated from places outside Africa. Darien LaBeach is the director of diversity at a marketing agency. He was born in Jamaica and raised in the United States. He identifies as Black, but not African American. "African American technically isn't even what I am," he says.

"I'm a Jamaican-born Black person, but [people call me] African American because of where I live." He says about Blackness, "We are all connected. Our experiences are different, but we are still linked."[5] There is no single way to define Black culture. But it is a way Black Americans can express their shared experiences, heritage, and sense of identity.

LANGUAGE AND LITERATURE

Many enslaved Africans came from countries with oral traditions. Enslaved people were not allowed to read and write. As a result, many stories, histories, and traditions were passed down orally. A mix of languages and **dialects** shaped unique ways of speaking in Black communities.

Spoken word poetry is a popular expression that combines speaking and performing poetry live in front a crowd. Amanda Gorman is a National Youth Poet Laureate and spoken word poet.

Today, African American Vernacular English (AAVE) is recognized as its own style of speaking and writing.

The Harlem Renaissance took place from 1918 to 1937. This was a period of Black creative expression. It was centered in Harlem, New York. Writers challenged racist **stereotypes**. They wrote about their experiences as Black Americans.

Important writers included Zora Neale Hurston and Langston Hughes. The Harlem Renaissance paved the way for some of the greatest American writers. These include James Baldwin, Maya Angelou, and Toni Morrison.

MUSIC AND DANCE

Black Americans have used music to worship, celebrate, and survive difficult times. African instruments, Black culture, and Black musicians have influenced almost every genre of American music. Ragtime and blues were popular in the 1800s. Jazz emerged in the early 1900s. Musicians such as Louis Armstrong and Ella Fitzgerald changed American music. Other more modern genres of music have been defined by Black artists. These include R&B, rock, funk, and Motown. They also include pop, hip-hop, and rap. Michael Jackson, Prince, and Beyoncé are some of the most successful musicians of all time.

Beyoncé is the most decorated singer in Grammy history.

Different styles of dance reflect these musical traditions. Tap dance has roots in African step dance. Enslaved people developed it further on plantations. Jazz dance came from Black social dances in the 1930s and 1940s. Hip-hop dance, music, and culture emerged in the 1970s. Young artists developed it. They were responding to crime, violence, and poverty in areas such as the Bronx, New York.

STYLE AND EXPRESSION

Fashion is a form of expression. It has also been used for resistance and protest. Black fashion affects trends in the fashion industry. Streetwear is a casual, comfortable style. It includes baggy clothes, graphic tees, and hats. This clothing reflects

Air Jordans became popular on basketball courts and in hip-hop circles.

the hip-hop and skate culture of Harlem and Brooklyn. Athleisure blends athletic and casual clothing. It was made popular by Black athletes. Sneaker culture is an example of both styles. Shoes can show personal style and social status. The Nike Air Jordans helped sneaker culture explode

Locs are a natural hairstyle created by tightly coiling or twisting hair.

in popularity. Basketball player Michael Jordan partnered with Nike in the 1980s. He wore Air Jordans on the court. They became popular off the court, too.

Hair is an important part of Black identity. Natural hair has been a target of discrimination for Black people. But it's also been a symbol of protest and self-acceptance. Some protective hair styles have been passed down through history. These include Bantu knots and cornrows. Hairstyles such as the Afro expressed Black resistance during the Civil Rights Movement.

Many Black Americans are pressured to relax or straighten their natural hair. This is especially true for women and girls. But the natural hair movement has led to more women wearing their textured hair naturally. Author Monica Millner writes, "I feel that kinks, curls, or tight coils in Afro hair is beautiful and unique. No other race on this planet has hair like ours—that makes me proud."[6]

CHAPTER THREE

RELIGIONS

Ninety-seven percent of Black Americans believe in God or a higher power. This is compared to 90 percent of the overall population. About 60 percent of Black Americans say religion is very important in their lives.

The majority of Black Americans are Christian. Most are Protestant. Others identify as Catholic or other denominations.

Christmas is an important holiday for Christians.

Some Bibles published for enslaved people removed the Exodus story and other stories of people in bondage seeking freedom.

THE BLACK CHURCH

Enslaved Africans had their own faiths. About a quarter were Muslim. Others practiced different spiritual traditions. Many enslavers encouraged or forced slaves to convert to Christianity. Parts of Christianity and the Bible were used to justify slavery. Enslavers and pastors quoted passages such as Ephesians 6:5. It states, “Slaves, obey your earthly masters.”[7]

Other parts of the Bible offered comfort. Many enslaved people saw themselves in the Exodus story. Egyptians enslaved the Israelites. God helped the Israelites escape from Egypt. They were led by Moses. The story became a symbol for escape to freedom.

Black Americans formed their own churches. Black ministers encouraged their congregations to worship in ways that felt comfortable for them. Many services included more traditional African customs of worship. These involved clapping, singing, and dancing.

Much later, the Black church became a place of protest for the Civil

Rights Movement. Churches played a major role in organizing protests. For many Black Americans, Christianity represents freedom, hope, and justice. The church has a complicated history. But Black churches have served as places of community. They allow Black Americans to worship, grieve, and celebrate together.

Rastafari

Rastafari was created in Jamaica in the 1930s. The religion follows Biblical stories. It also includes meditation and other ceremonies. Rastafari teaches that people of African descent are exiles. They are meant to return to Ethiopia in Africa. Reggae music was inspired by Rastafari. This music was made popular by musician Bob Marley.

Some female Muslims wear a head covering called a hijab.

ISLAM

Islam is the next most popular religion among Black Americans. Black Africans were likely the first Muslims to live in

North America. Some enslaved people refused to convert to Christianity. They held on to their Islamic faith.

Islam had a revival in the 1960s. Malcolm X saw the religion as a way of embracing his African heritage. "In Islam a man is honored as a human being and not measured by the color of his skin," he said.[8] Many Black Americans converted after reading Malcom X's autobiography.

VOODOO

Other African religious traditions found their way to America. New Orleans, Louisiana, is known for Voodoo. Voodoo has roots in West African religious practices.

Enslaved Black people mixed with Creole, French, and Spanish people of

The New Orleans Historic Voodoo Museum teaches visitors about the religion.

the French Louisiana colony. The religion evolved. It grew more when Haitian immigrants settled in New Orleans around 1810. Haitians brought their own traditions, called Vodou. New Orleans Voodoo blended West African spiritual beliefs with Catholicism.

CHAPTER FOUR

BLACK AMERICANS TODAY

In 2024, Black Americans made up around 14 percent of the US population. That's about 48 million people. The majority of Black Americans live in the South.

Black Americans have made incredible contributions to American culture. But **disparities** continue to exist between Black and white Americans. Many are the result of discrimination throughout history.

Black Americans play an important role in US government, culture, and public life.

WEALTH DISPARITIES

Income is the amount of money someone earns. *Wealth* is the total value of someone's possessions. It can be built upon and passed down across generations. Alexandra Killewald is a professor. She studies inequality in the United States. "Today's [Black] adults and children are living with the legacy of discrimination, inequality, and exclusion, from slavery to . . . other discriminatory practices," she says. "And in turn, white Americans are benefiting from legacies of advantage."[9]

Racism has kept Black Americans from gathering the same wealth as white Americans. This has happened throughout US history. Redlining is one example. Redlining was a government practice.

In Saint Paul, Minnesota, Rondo was a thriving Black neighborhood. But in the 1950s, officials allowed Interstate 94 to be built through it. One in eight Black homeowners in Saint Paul lost their homes.

It labeled Black neighborhoods as "hazardous" or "high risk." Banks worried about giving loans for homes in these areas. This prevented many Black people from owning homes. It also meant Black neighborhoods received less government support. Redlining began in the 1930s. It continued for decades. Its impact is still felt today. In 2020, only 44 percent of Black families owned their own home. Meanwhile, 75 percent of white families owned their own home.

Wealth affects opportunities in other areas of society. Schools are usually funded by property taxes. This means schools in wealthier areas often get more funding. Schools in Black communities usually have fewer resources. They have lower-paid

Areas without access to fresh foods, especially fruits and vegetables, are known as food deserts.

teachers who may be less experienced. This can lead to lower test scores and graduation rates for Black students.

Where people live can also affect their health. Poorer areas often have less access to fresh food. They also have fewer outdoor spaces. The United Church of Christ (UCC) studies environmental injustice. Environmental injustice is when environmental issues affect some groups more than others. These issues include water, soil, and air pollution. The UCC studied toxic waste sites in the United States. It found that most people living near toxic waste sites were people of color. These areas may be polluted or have lower air quality. This can lead to more health risks.

Those with less wealth are also less likely to access high-quality health care. But studies show wealth and education don’t prevent poor care for Black Americans. For centuries, medical schools taught about biological differences between Black and white people. These were false. But the myths live on. Some doctors think Black people feel less pain. Black patients may struggle to get pain medicine as a result. Discovering an illness early can make it easier to treat. But Black patients report doctors not taking them seriously. Some doctors dismiss symptoms as something minor. But the symptoms actually point to major illnesses. This causes delays in treatment. These delays can be deadly.

Tennis superstar Serena Williams had complications after giving birth to her daughter. She recognized symptoms from a past medical episode, but the nurses dismissed her concerns. Williams's story highlighted the health care problems many Black women face.

FIGHTING FOR CHANGE

Studies show that Black Americans are killed by police at twice the rate of white Americans. In 2020, police arrested a Black man named George Floyd in

Minneapolis, Minnesota. Officer Derek Chauvin held his knee on Floyd's neck. He kept it there for more than 8 minutes. Floyd said he could not breathe. But Chauvin did not release him. Floyd died. Onlookers recorded Floyd's murder. They shared it online. It caused protests worldwide. This drew attention to other areas of racial injustice. Ilhan Omar is a US representative from Minnesota. She spoke about the protests in 2020. She said, "It's a call for justice. . . . It's a call for our humanity to be recognized."[10] The officers involved in Floyd's death were charged with murder. They were sentenced to prison.

Since 2020, thirty states have passed police reform laws. Other communities have funded mental health, violence prevention, and counseling programs. These can be more effective than police intervention.

Black American history is American history. Black Americans helped build the nation into a global superpower. But they were denied their share of progress. Despite centuries of suffering and racism, Black Americans are still fighting. They work to make a country that offers liberty and justice for all.

The Black Vote

Many Black Americans still face barriers in voting. Stacey Abrams served in the Georgia House of Representatives. She founded the organization Fair Fight Action. It works to expand voting access. Her work inspired an estimated 800,000 people in Georgia to register to vote in 2020.

GLOSSARY

abolitionists
people who worked to end slavery

boycotts
refusals to buy or participate in something until demands are met

dialects
particular forms of language used by specific groups

discrimination
treating a person or group worse than others due to differences

disparities
unfair differences in treatment

economy
the structure around money, trade, and industry in a country

immigrants
people who come to live permanently in a country they are not originally from

segregated
intentionally separated, often by race

stereotypes
oversimplified generalizations of people in a specific group

SOURCE NOTES

INTRODUCTION: CELEBRATING BLACK HERITAGE

1. Quoted in Terry Tang, "The Beginner's Guide to Celebrating Juneteenth," *NBC Washington*, June 19, 2024. www.nbcwashington.com.

CHAPTER ONE: HISTORY OF BLACK AMERICANS

2. "The United States Constitution," *National Constitution Center*, n.d. http://constitutioncenter.org.

3. "Transcript of Barack Obama's Victory Speech," *NPR*, November 5, 2008. www.npr.org.

CHAPTER TWO: CULTURE AND TRADITIONS

4. Quoted in Cydney Adams, "Not All Black People Are African American. Here's the Difference," *CBS News*, June 18, 2020. www.cbsnews.com.

5. Quoted in Adams, "Not All Black People Are African American."

6. Quoted in Deana-Rae Weatherly, "Strands of Inspiration: Exploring Black Identities Through Hair," *National Museum of African American History & Culture*, August 16, 2023. http://nmaahc.si.edu.

CHAPTER THREE: RELIGIONS

7. "Ephesians 6:5–9 (New International Version)," *Bible Gateway*, n.d. www.biblegateway.com.

8. "Malcolm X," *Robert Penn Warren's Who Speaks for the Negro? An Archival Collection*, n.d. https://whospeaks.library.vanderbilt.edu.

CHAPTER FOUR: BLACK AMERICANS TODAY

9. Quoted in Liz Mineo, "Racial Wealth Gap May Be a Key to Other Inequities," *The Harvard Gazette*, June 3, 2021. http://news.harvard.edu.

10. Quoted in "What They Said: Leaders React to George Floyd Death," *The Minnesota Star Tribune*, May 28, 2020. www.startribune.com.

FOR FURTHER RESEARCH

BOOKS

J. Boney, *Kwanzaa and Other African American Holidays*. BrightPoint Press, 2026.

Duchess Harris with R. L. Van, *Race and Policing in Modern America*. Abdo Publishing, 2021.

Gail Terp, *Climate and Environmental Injustice*. BrightPoint Press, 2023.

INTERNET SOURCES

"From Slavery to Freedom in Colonial Times," *PBS Learning Media*, n.d. http://pbslearningmedia.org.

Kemisa Kassa, "Juneteenth," *NCpedia*, 2023. www.ncpedia.org.

"Network to Freedom: Underground Railroad Locations Map," *National Park Service*, n.d. http://nps.maps.arcgis.com.

WEBSITES

Black History Month

http://blackhistorymonth.gov

Every February is Black History Month. This website features articles and resources to explore Black history, art, images, and more.

NAACP

http://naacp.org

The NAACP is an organization that fights for racial justice. Explore current issues of racial equality and resources to combat racism.

National Museum of African American History and Culture

http://nmaahc.si.edu/learn/students

This branch of the Smithsonian Museum has online libraries of stories, articles, and photographs about African American history.

INDEX

IMAGE CREDITS

Cover: © Wavebreak Media/Shutterstock Images
5: © alyssasieb/Nappy
7: © Erin Scott/Biden White House
8: © Chandler West/Biden White House
10: © Red Line Editorial
11: © AnnaStills/Shutterstock Images
13: © Kosoff/Shutterstock Images
14: © Randy Duchaine/Alamy
17: © Library of Congress
19: © Library of Congress
20: © Library of Congress
23: © Bettmann/Getty Images
25: © David L. Harris/Library of Congress
26: © Pete Souza/Obama White House
29: © AnnaStills/Shutterstock Images
33: © Maxim Elramsisy/Shutterstock Images
35: © Kathy Hutchins/Shutterstock Images
37: © ShamAn77/Shutterstock Images
38: © RootedColors/Nappy
41: © NappyStock/Nappy
42: © Pressmaster/Shutterstock Images
45: © adriaticfoto/Shutterstock Images
47: © Ritu Manoj Jethani/Shutterstock Images
49: © Gorodenkoff/Shutterstock Images
51: © Steve Heap/Shutterstock Images
52: © Hryshchyshen Serhii/Shutterstock Images
55: © Tinseltown/Shutterstock Images

ABOUT THE AUTHOR

Emma Kaiser is a writer and educator from Minnesota. She has a master of fine arts in creative writing from the University of Minnesota, and her writing has appeared in many magazines and publications. She is the author of a number of other nonfiction books for students.